Simply Modern Life

To Sue,
Best Wishes,
Claire B.

SIMPLY MODERN LIFE

A Collection of Poetry

Claire Baldry
Illustrated by Amber Gee

Matador
9 Priory Business Park,
Wistow Road, Kibworth Beauchamp,
Leicestershire. LE8 0RX
Tel: 0116 279 2299
Email: books@troubador.co.uk
Web: www.troubador.co.uk/matador
Twitter: @matadorbooks

ISBN 978 1789015 324

British Library Cataloguing in Publication Data.
A catalogue record for this book is available from the British Library.

Typeset in 11pt Minion Pro by Troubador Publishing Ltd, Leicester, UK

Matador is an imprint of Troubador Publishing Ltd

For Doreen Mills, Julie Rossall, Will,
and Spanners 1, 3 and 4

About the Author and Illustrator

Sixty-three year old Claire Baldry retired from her career as a Headteacher and English Advisor in 2008. She is now an established writer, blogger, performance poet and public speaker in her home county of East Sussex. Claire has published four previous booklets of poetry, and more recently her debut novel 'Different Genes'. 'Simply Modern Life' is the first collection of poetry in which Claire has collaborated with illustrator, Amber Gee.

Twenty-four year old Amber Gee was born in West Sussex. She graduated from university with an upper second degree in English Literature in 2016 and now works as a full-time care worker whilst pursuing her creative art work in her spare time. Diagnosed with SLD, Amber describes herself as "easily distracted with poor organisational skills". At school Amber's teachers tried to explain to her that not every piece of schoolwork needed an illustration, but Amber refused to wait for Art to crop up on the timetable. She says it was completely impossible to survive Double Maths without some sort of creative outlet for the stress it was causing her. She spent much of her time in school missing PE and creating art projects. Amber now takes a sketchbook with her wherever she goes, but loses it so often that she is more likely to be found doodling on an old train ticket.

Claire says "It's ironic that, as a retired headteacher, I find myself working alongside someone who found it so difficult to adapt to the demands of the British Education system. Amber is a prime example of how individual talent should be nurtured, rather than pigeon-holed into an inflexible curriculum. Working with Amber has been both frustrating and inspirational. Her lateral thinking and wonderful drawings have added a unique dimension to my poems."

Contents

I Rhyme

I rhyme
Out of time
Deliver rendition
In couplet tradition
Unknown by the media
Unlisted in wikipedia
Unfollowed on twitter
Unloved but not bitter
Past my life sell by date
Written decades too late
To be heard in a slam
Or a poetry jam
But I make no apology
For my rhymed poetology
More compulsive than fiction
Rhyming is an addiction

Peace on the Train

We are heading up to London on the fifteen thirty-four,
Our coats are on the rack above, our cases on the floor,
We read our books in silence, 'til an irritating tone,
Rings out from three seats further back,
and Julie's on the phone

"Hello there, yes it's Julie!"
"Is she deaf?" asks my friend, Jane,
"Yes, I'm on my way to London,"
(Damn, she's staying on the train)
"No, I've lots of time to natter,
We can chat 'til Clapham Junction"
And we hope her battery fades,
So that her phone will cease to function

"Did you buy that bright red sofa?
Mine's a lovely shade of pink,
Will it match new purple curtains,
Or bright orange, what d'you think?
I'm going to buy a bedspread for my uncle's Spanish villa"
Jane turns to me and whispers,
"Would they notice if I kill her?"
"Hang on, Sarah, there's a tunnel
For a moment I'll be quiet"
"Just as well," I mumble softly,
"Or the passengers will riot"
"Yes, I'm back now, did you miss me?
Oh, you've gone, that is a shame"
But we all sigh with relief, that we no longer hear her name
We sit noiselessly to Gatwick,
Watch the signs for Croydon pass,
Smile with sympathy in tolerance
At the teacher with his class
Then a young man joins at Clapham,
Rhythm pounding from his ears
Jane hands over several tissues
To mop up my desperate tears
I meet my Aunt in London,
As I leave the railway line
Auntie asks, "How was your journey?"
I say "Absolutely fine"

The Good Old Days

Let's blame...............mobile phones
For the problems in society
For weak communication
And decline in our propriety
Let's blame mobile phones

Let's blame...............poor spelling
And misuse of the apostrophe
For the loss of moral values
And a breakdown in the family
Let's blame poor spelling

Let's blame...............kilograms
And pints replaced by litres
For obesity in children
For greedy banks and cheaters
Let's blame kilograms

Let's blame...............technology,
Science, freedom, innovation
For the challenges which face
The changing context of our nation
Let's blame technology

Let's bring back national service,
Let's restrict freedom of thought
Blame the schools for bad behaviour
And the way our kids are taught
Let's bring back national service

Let's go back to the 'Good Old Days'
When poor people knew their place
When we had no regulation
Over gender, faith or race
Let's go back to the 'Good Old Days'

Let's disregard advances,
Central heating, living longer,
Global travel, vaccination,
Roles for women which are stronger,
Let's disregard advances

Let's ignore all history lessons
Paint a future clothed in dread
Blame all progress for our troubles
Worship backwardness instead

The Gang are Feeling Cool

Abbie came home in tears today,
She said she hated school,
The children wouldn't play with her,
Or let her catch the ball,
They didn't like her gingham dress,
The way she loved her books,
They said that once outside the shops,
She gave them funny looks

Johnny came home from work today,
He said he felt quite stressed,
The office staff ignored him,
When they stopped to take a rest
They didn't like his posh accent,
They laughed behind his back,
He thought they might report him,
Then the boss gave him the sack

Billy went online today,
The gang watched him arrive
They lay in wait to harass him,
So his esteem would dive.
Now Billy's got depression,
While Abbie's missing school,
And Johnny's on the whisky,
But the gang are feeling cool

No Room at the Inn

"Knock, knock" said the traveller,
"Who's there?" I replied
He sat on the dockside,
Spoke out as he cried

"I am just a sad migrant,
Homeless and poor,
I have fled from oppression,
From violence and war

My house is destroyed,
My children are dead,
I'll work for a living,
Could you lend me a bed?"

"So sorry, young man,
But you're well out of order,
Our country is full,
We have closed down our border

We espouse British values,
We give generous aid,
Our record of tolerance
Puts others in shade

We need our resources,
Our Doctors work hard,
You will take all our jobs,
Grab an NHS card

Go beg somewhere different,
Scavenge food from a bin,
Make your home in the gutter,
There's no room at our inn

Mobility Rap

I used to drive a moped
Then upgraded to a car
I took my turn on school runs
And collected kids from far
I chauffeured family outings
In a space wagon quite maxi
And sometimes I complained my car
Was treated like a taxi

One day we packed the motor
Set the sat nav for the lakes
A lorry swerved before me
And I pressed hard on the brakes
The impact shook my body
For a moment I touched hell
We all survived the crisis
But my legs don't work so well

I struggled with my ego
Felt a massive loss of pride
My chauffeur days were over
Now I'd have to seek a ride
I gave myself a lecture
Did a search on the computer
Reinvented independence
With a bright electric scooter

It isn't supersonic,
You can watch how slow it goes
I ride along the pavement
And avoid the shoppers' toes
But now I have my wheels back
With a battery and a hooter
I'm the speed queen of the neighbours
On my lovely bright red scooter

The AGM

(To the tune of 'John Brown's Body')

There's a rumbling from the back row,
There's vibration in the aisle,
There is snuffling in the distance,
As the Chairman grabs his file,
We all turn to look behind us,
As his wife gives him a nudge,
But George goes snoring on

CHORUS

Glory, Glory, Hallelujah,
Meetings can be so peculiar,
Glory, Glory, Hallelujah,
Another AGM

The Chairman taps the table,
We go quiet, as we've been taught,
It is time to call on Hazel for the treasurer's report,
She describes our lavish spending
On the biscuits and the tea,
But George goes snoring on

CHORUS

Hazel asks for any questions,
We so hope there will be none,
Then dear Arthur stands to query,
And an answer must be done,
He has noticed tuppence missing,
She admits the coin was lost,
But George goes snoring on

CHORUS

Then the secretary rises
To read out a lengthy tome,
We all hide our slight relief,
She's left her spectacles at home,
Beryl tells us all of illness,
Doreen says we should send flowers,
But George goes snoring on

CHORUS

"Is there any other business?
Olive, you have a request,"
"Yes, the ladies making tea, as always,
Do their very best,
Though they often miss the speaker,
Could we not take it in turns?"
But George goes snoring on

CHORUS

Then we chat about the heating,
And noisy hot air blower,
That we really need a microphone,
And speakers who talk slower,
We could do with some more members
For our rather small committee,
But George goes snoring on.

CHORUS

"Thank you everyone for coming,
Now it's tea and raffle time,"
I look down at my three tickets,
Hope the winning number's mine,
It is blue, six and four hundred,
That's the number bought by George,
But George goes snoring on

CHORUS

Visiting the Nurse

(To be sung to the tune of 'Away in a Manger')

I went to the Doctor's, I tried not to fret,
The Nurse likes to see you, the older you get
She asked about lifestyle, how often I fry,
She checked my blood pressure and my BMI

I cut down the units, I went for a swim,
I wore sporty footwear, I tried to look slim,
I chose lightweight clothing, not tops I look fat in,
If the blood test is high, she might give me a statin

I went to the Doctor's close by Manor Barn,
I missed out on breakfast, that did me no harm,
Results come tomorrow, a phone call I'll make,
If I get the all clear, then I'll eat a big cake

The Insulin Pump

Chris has Diabetes,
It really isn't fun,
Forever testing levels,
As, of course, he's my 'Type 1'

Needles in his fingers,
Injections in his tum,
He's jabbed himself so often
That his finger tips are numb

And people ask daft questions
Like "Should he be eating that?"
"Yes, he does know what he's doing,
And not all Type 1s are fat!"

Sometimes I give him glucogel,
At night when he feels rough,
He really doesn't like it,
Well, have you tasted that stuff?

Twice a year he visits outpatients
Not always willingly
They measure his cholesterol
And his HbA1c

They test his pee, and poke his feet,
And take his weight and height
And ask him endless questions,
And he has to be polite

But after years of needles,
He is now blue-tooth connected
To a pump with plastic piping
So his life is far less wretched

There is still a lot of testing,
But he has achieved one goal,
He is now the proud possessor,
Of his own remote control.

Ladies Who Sing

The choir of lovely ladies
Formed a line to take their chairs
Dressed in black with yellow 'kerchiefs,
They approached the stage in pairs

At the back were all the climbers,
Who could safely cope with height,
With the small ones in the front row,
As the space was rather tight

There were plenty of sopranos
Who could sing the notes in tune,
And rather fewer altos,
But their voices filled the room

And a lady in the corner,
Who had caused the group concern,
Whether she would ever manage to
Sing only when her turn

And the rather bossy Mary,
She told others what to do,
And dear Vera on the final seat,
As she might want the loo

And the 'Master' in his jacket,
Looking dapper as can be,
Pointing upwards with his baton,
Mouthing 'Please all look at me'

Then, dear Julie, in the middle,
Who had begged to join the choir,
Though her pitch was somewhat challenged,
When she tried to sing much higher

They had struggled with the crotchets,
Juggled quavers and repeats,
Felt depressed at their slow progress,
In the last rehearsal meets

But the Master tapped his baton,
Cast a glimpse towards the band,
And, as if they were one person,
The whole choir began to stand

Music sheets before them,
Eyes directed at their King,
He lifted up his baton and
The choir began to sing

Music filled the rafters
With a mellow sound so clear
And, as they reached their final notes,
The audience gave a cheer

The Harvest Assembly

"Next week we are holding a Harvest Assembly,
No, Jason, it isn't a bit like Wembley,
You all bring donations of packets and jars,
We put them in boxes and load up our cars,
We sing Autumn songs, now the days are quite short,
Show thanks for our food, by the gifts we have brought

No, I'm sorry, dear Jason, but this isn't funny,
Yes, of course, Tanya May, you can invite your mummy,
No, we can't eat the food, it is meant for the poor,
No, not even a bit, yes, of course, I am sure,
Can we sing about football? No, Jason, we can't,
Yes, of course, Tanya May, you can invite your Aunt

Have you all understood? Do you all have the note?
Have you fetched your book bags, remembered your coat?
Then it's hometime, dear children,
Jason, don't make me stern,
I am off to the staff room to dream of half-term

Choices

A parentless child hides from a sniper
in a distant land
She doesn't want ideology, only dinner

An elderly resident waits to be rescued
from an overflowing river
She wants electricity, not flooded carpets

Please don't ask me to choose
between the needs of humanity
Please don't bombard me with facebook messages
Please don't tell me what I should believe

I cannot choose

I ask only this

That the inadequate giving from my purse
Makes a difference
That my money is used for dinner and education
And effective flood defence
That I do not donate to corruption or incompetence

That is my only choice

My Telephone Week

He called me on a Monday,
Said his name was Guy,
Told me of the refund
I could get for PPI

The phone rang twice on Tuesday,
The lady's name was Dee,
She spoke of eco matters,
How my boiler would be free

On Wednesday I was worried
By an accident I'd had,
The insurance chap who phoned me,
Was convinced the wounds were bad

On Thursday my computer
Had a virus, warned the man,
If I'd just pay an online fee,
They'd do a special scan

Friday's call brought surveys,
Detailed finance questionnaires,
Do they really need my passwords
And the numbers of my shares?

Saturday at 6 am,
The voice said not to fret,
A special deal was waiting
That would clear me of my debt

Sunday…...it's so quiet,
I am sitting with a book,
Sunday is my day of rest,
The phone is off the hook

Our Digital House

This is the digital house that we built.
This is the room in the digital house that we built.
This is the phone in the room in the digital house that we built.

This is the screen of the phone which she read in despair in a room all alone in the digital house that we built.
This is the joke which was no longer funny on the screen of the phone which she read in despair in a room all alone in the digital house that we built.

These are the tears of regret at the joke which was no longer funny on the screen of the phone which she read in despair in a room all alone in the digital house that we built.
This is the mother who wept with the tears of regret at the joke which was no longer funny on the screen of the phone which she read in despair in a room all alone in the digital house that we built.

This is the overdosed girl who was lost to the mother who wept with the tears of regret at the joke which was no longer funny on the screen of the phone which she read in despair in a room all alone in the digital house that we built.
This is the box of the overdosed girl who was lost to the mother who wept with the tears of regret at the joke which was no longer funny on the screen of the phone which she read in despair in a room all alone in the digital house that we built.

This is the hearse that transported the box of the overdosed girl who was lost to the mother who wept with the tears of regret at the joke which was no longer funny on the screen of the phone which she read in despair in a room all alone in the digital house that we built.

The Inspection

Ofsted came Tuesday,
Sir gave us a talk,
How we must be polite,
Never run, always walk

Remember our targets,
'Don't shout' Billy jones,
Play nicely at playtimes,
Store away mobile phones

Bring all our PE kit,
Arrive well on time,
Listen to teachers,
Form an orderly line

The Inspectors came promptly,
Wearing suits and grey hair,
Scribbled notes in assembly,
We tried not to stare

They watched us in lessons,
Tried cook's treacle pud',
And, when the report came,
It said we were good

Well, we already knew that,
'Cause we do try our best,
But at least now our teachers
Are not quite so stressed

The Alien School

There was once a school of aliens,
Who lived beyond the stars,
They studied distant travel
To a planet beyond Mars

Their project had a focus,
Find the perfect destination,
For long journeys in a space ship
To a Milky Way sensation

The students, in an essay,
Took great care with each word written,
Told how Earthlings came from East and West
To seek a place called Britain

"Why is UK so attractive?"
Asked the strict galactic teachers,
"We have heard it's full of teashops,
Rainy days are frequent features

And the inmates dig their gardens,
Eat strong curry with real ale,
Get obsessive over football,
Protest hard to 'Save the Whale'

Worship 'heroes', such as Churchill,
Lady Thatcher, husband Dennis,
Watch a ball game, known as cricket,
'Men in White' whilst playing tennis

What on earth makes this place special?
Is it Harrods, M&S?
Or the Queen and her attendants?
BBC or NHS?"

"More than that" young aliens stated,
"UK is the place to reach,
They have fish and chips and custard,
Dr Who, …Oh and free speech!"

Counting the Hits

I'm sitting on the sofa
In my comfy Bexhill home,
Staring at the small screen,
As I upload to my phone

I thought I'd go live on the web,
It's better than a selfie,
If loads of people watch me,
Then I might become quite wealthy

I'm counting hits on You Tube,
To date I've thirty-four,
I want to be a film star,
So I'm going to need some more

I long to make a fortune,
For my online fame to spiral,
I hoped they'd love my poems,
And my rhyming would go viral

I shared the link on facebook
With the folk I call my friends,
I checked the google figures
And the analytic trends

I have a few subscribers
At this time it's less than twenty,
But I am optimistic that
One day it will be plenty

So now I sit here waiting
In the hope the hits will spike,
That hoards of fans will watch me
And then click to say they like

Beware of the Trolls

They like to jab a needle in a touchy space,
An online provocation right against your face,
They seek your darkest corners and invade your souls,
They are nasty, wormlike phantoms,
Called the internet trolls

They post a ghastly picture, then they disappear,
Swamp your page with troubles and invade your fear,
They tunnel under virtual ground, sneaky Facebook moles,
They are shadows in your backyard,
Called the internet trolls

They gather several emails, so can change their name,
This lets them work in secret, they can hide their shame,
You'll hardly ever spot them, as they chase their goals,
They are damaged friendless beings,
Called the internet trolls

So, children, in your nightmares,
Filled with thoughts you dread,
Be grateful for the monsters underneath your bed,
They will teach you self- protection
They will keep you whole,
For the time you meet a demon,
Called the internet troll

My Facebook Friend

(To the tune of 'I had a Little Nut Tree')

I had a friend on Facebook,
He said he was my mate,
He phoned me on a Tuesday
And asked me for a date

He said he was a soldier,
Had served across the sea,
And hinted, if we once met up,
That he would marry me

I found his words a comfort,
No longer felt a wreck,
He needed cash for his plane fare,
I sent him a large cheque

Alas he caught a virus,
It isn't very funny,
But I am sure he'll visit soon,
Because he has my money

The Egerton Witch

Remember the tale of Rapunzel
In a tower with her long flowing hair
Locked away 'til a prince came to save her,
Otherwise, she might still be in there?

The old witch was then stuck in the castle,
But a letter arrived in the post,
Telling her of compulsory purchase
That she would be rehoused by the coast

So the witch packed her spells and her potions,
With relief that a builder should bother
To arrange for her paid relocation
To a council owned turret in Rother

The removal men brought a large ladder,
Helped her climb from her home in the dark,
Sat her down in the back of their lorry,
'Til it stopped right by Egerton Park

She stared at the tower in the water,
And quickly came up with a plan
To make use of her knowledge of magic
To downsize as far as she can

She sipped from a test tube of potion
A murky and fizzy green drink
It worked on herself and her luggage,
And everything started to shrink

Then she borrowed a boat from the kiosk,
Packed it full of her tables and chairs,
Sailed across in one go to the folly,
And climbed up the miniature stairs

So if you go walking one evening
In the moonlight when moorhens roam free,
Listen out for a voice from the turret,
As it might be an invite to tea

But beware of the tiny old lady,
Who looks out for heads full of long hair,
If she calls out, it's best to ignore her,
Or you'll find yourself looked up in there

Two Men in a Boat

"What did you do, Dad, to stop feeling shame,
When the sea levels rose, and the waves finally came,
Before the great flood?"

"The problem was global, our actions too late,
We were busy existing, ignoring our fate,
Before the great flood

We blamed the plantations, third world, the Chinese,
We starved the poor people who cut down the trees,
Before the great flood

We wanted cheap food in order to thrive,
Public transport was slow, so we all chose to drive,
Before the great flood

Wind turbines were ugly, so we sent them away,
We resorted to fracking on recycling day,
Before the great flood"

"Did you use little shops and support local craft,
Pay an income to those who helped build our life raft,
Before the great flood?"

And the Dad shook his head,
Blamed world leaders and science,
Never seeing a need for his own self-reliance,
Before the great flood

They sailed to the sunset in the warm smoky air,
The son full of wonder that his Dad didn't care,
Before the great flood

Side By Side

Side by side,
Fingers touching,
We breathed the air of our life,
Husband, sister, friend, companion,
Mother, brother, work-mate, wife

Day by day,
Forward together,
Slow start, then a sprint,
With joyful thoughts and solemn moods,
We left a gift or a faint handprint

One by one
Living and learning,
We made a difference, explored the view,
Then, in no particular order,
Our souls were placed in a final queue

Little by little,
Hands moved apart,
You slipped away, as the door opened wide,
You passed over the step, outline blurred,
Took your place on the other side

See you there